# BROWNIE SCOUT HANDBOOK

*Girl Scouts of the United States of America*

830 THIRD AVENUE, NEW YORK 22, N. Y.

CATALOG NO. 20-110, PRICE 50 CENTS

*First Impression, December, 1951*

*Seventeenth Impression, June, 1959*



***Printed in the United States of America***

***Designed by Peter Oldenburg***

# Table of Contents

Dear Brownie Scout:

This is your own handbook. It tells you who the Brownie Scouts are and why they are called Brownies. It tells about Brownie Scout troops and the good times you have when you belong to one. It explains what you do to become a Brownie Scout. It tells you how you help to make your troop a good one.

The book is full of things girls your age like to do and how to do them. They are fun to do at troop meetings and at home. They help you learn to be a useful person.

Many Brownies have told us what they want in this book for all Brownie Scouts in the United States of America. We hope you like it and enjoy being a Brownie Scout so much that you will want to go on being a Girl Scout.

RAY MITCHELL

THIS BOOK was written by **Ray Mitchell,** *Brownie Scout Adviser, Program Department.* The pictures were drawn by **Ruth Wood,** *artist.*

# Brownie Scouts

BROWNIE SCOUTS are the Girl Scouts who are seven, eight, and nine years old. When you are a Brownie, you have a good time and learn how to help other people. You belong to a Brownie Scout troop. It meets once a week. The troop is your club with friends your own age. Two grown-up leaders belong to the troop too.

There are Brownie Scouts all over the United States and all over the world. They make the same Promise in their own language and do many of the same things everywhere.

*Brownies in France—Jeannettes*

*Brownies in England*

*Brownies in India—Bulbuls*

*Brownies in Brazil—Fadas (Fairies)*

### The Name Brownies

Brownie Scouts were named Brownies by the man who started the Boy Scouts and Girl Scouts. He is called the Founder of Scouting. His name was Robert Baden-Powell. He lived in England.

He knew many stories about the brownies or "little people of old England." They would come into a house at night and help while the family was asleep. The Founder thought Brownies would be a good name for girls who like to be useful as well as to play.

He took the name from a story called "The Brownies." You may read it in a book for yourself or hear it at your troop meeting.

## Our Girl Scout Founder

The Founder of the Girl Scouts in the United States of America was Mrs. Juliette Gordon Low. She liked girls and knew what they liked. Her home was in England part of the time. She knew Lord Robert Baden-Powell and helped him with the Girl Scouts there.

Mrs. Low knew the girls in this country would like to be Girl Scouts too. She came back to her home in Savannah, Georgia, and started the Girl Scouts. She helped make it possible for girls all over the world to be friends.

# How You Become a Brownie Scout

WHEN YOU join a Brownie Scout troop, you join the Girl Scouts of the United States of America. You are a member of all the Girl Scouts.

To be a Brownie Scout you must be seven, eight, or nine years old. You have finished the first grade at school and are in the second, third, or fourth grade. You will belong to a troop with girls who live in your neighborhood or go to the same school, church, or synagogue that you do. Your mother will talk to the leader of the troop you will join.

These are the things you do to become a Brownie Scout:

**1.** ***Attend Four Meetings of the Brownie Scout Troop.*** You attend four meetings so you can find out about Brownie Scouts. You make friends with all the girls in the troop. You get ready to make the Brownie Scout Promise. It may take longer than four meetings if the troop is a new one.

Brownies have such a good time they are glad when

the troop meeting day comes every week. You have many ideas when you get together and at the troop meeting you can do the things you like best.

Brownie troops like to fix up their troop meeting place so it will be their own troop room while they are in it. You can do this at troop meetings and take turns doing the housekeeping every week.

Troops meet on the day that suits everybody best at the same time each week. Your meetings are not very long but if you are on time you won't miss any of the fun. You like it better when you are there to do your part in everything and the other girls can count on you.

All the girls in the troop and the leaders decide together what you are going to do. Sometimes you just play. Or you may be very busy doing something you like or learning something you never tried before. You have a good time together.

2. ***Pay Your National Membership Dues.***

You pay one dollar every year to belong to the Brownie Scouts. These are your national membership dues. Everybody who belongs to a club or organization pays her part to help run it. You will need troop dues to help run your troop too, but this dollar is for being a member of the Girl Scouts of the United States of America. All the Girl Scouts in the country pay membership dues so they can have a troop. Only the members can wear the pin and the uniform.

All of you bring your membership dues to the troop. Your leader sends your money to Girl Scout National Headquarters and your name is put on the roll with all the Brownie Scouts in the United States. You get a membership card—a new one every year—to show that you belong. The troop gets a troop certificate.

GIRL SCOUTS OF THE UNITED STATES OF AMERICA
830 Third Ave., New York 22, N. Y.
CERTIFICATE OF MEMBERSHIP
Girl Scout

is a member of the Girl Scout movement.
This membership expires: (Month) ______ (Year) ______
Troop Number ______ Program ______
City or town ______ State ______
Council ______

JULIETTE LOW, Founder

President

3. ***Make Your Brownie Scout Promise.***

*I promise to do my best to love God and my country, to help other people every day, especially those at home.*

Every girl who becomes a Brownie Scout makes this Promise. You are not a Brownie just at troop meetings but all the time and the Promise will help you be one.

When you promise to *do your best,* you mean you will really try hard to do as well as *you* can. This is more than just doing what someone else tells you to do. You may forget sometimes but you can keep on trying.

Talk with your leader and your mother and father and the other Brownies in your troop about what you mean when you say you will do your best to love God and your country.

You can think of many ways yourself to help other people, especially those at home. You can make your family glad there is a Brownie at your house.

## You Are Invested

Your leader will tell you what it means to be invested. When you have been to as many meetings as you need in order to learn what it means to be a Brownie Scout, you are ready to belong. You have made friends with all the girls in the troop. You have paid your membership dues to the Girl Scouts of the United States of America. You know the Brownie Scout Promise.

You make your Promise at the troop meeting. Then your leader *invests* you. She pins your Brownie Scout pin on the right-hand side of your collar as soon as you have made your Promise. After the leader and you salute each other or use the Girl Scout handshake, the troop may salute you. Or they may show in some other way what an important day this is for the troop. This is a ceremony and is called the *In-ves-ti-ture.* Now you are a Brownie Scout.

### The Brownie Scout Pin

This is your Brownie Scout pin. The brownie is on a trefoil. The trefoil is the symbol of Girl Scouting all over the world. You wear it to show that you are a Brownie and belong to the Girl Scouts.

### The Girl Scout Membership Star

This star means that you have been a member one year. You may buy one at the end of each year you have been a Brownie and pin it on your uniform pocket.

### The Brownie Scout Uniform

This is your Brownie uniform. You wear it to troop meetings, to school on meeting days and on special Brownie Scout occasions. You may wear it the day you are invested if your membership dues have been sent in.

**The Brownie Scout Salute**

This is the way you make the Brownie Scout salute. Your first two fingers held straight stand for the two parts of your Promise. You use the salute when you make your Promise and, if you are in uniform, when you see the Flag raised or lowered or passing by.

**The Greeting Sign**

This is the way you make the Brownie Scout greeting sign. You use it to greet other Brownies and Girl Scouts as a sign of friendship, in the way knights of old used to do.

**The Handshake**

This is the Girl Scout handshake. You salute with your right hand and shake hands with your left. Brownies and Girl Scouts use this handshake all over the world.

## The Girl Scout Motto

*"Be Prepared"*

This is the motto for all Girl Scouts. To be prepared means to be ready. When you learn the words in your spelling lesson, you are prepared for your class. When you know how to set the table, you are prepared to help your mother when she is busy getting dinner.

Girl Scouts learn to do things well so they will be prepared to do them in the right way at the right time. When something seems hard to do at first, you keep on trying until you satisfy *yourself* that you have done the best you can. Then you feel prepared to do it.

## The Girl Scout Slogan

***"Do a Good Turn Daily"***

"Doing a good turn" means doing something for somebody else without being asked or being paid for it. It is fun to surprise someone at home or at school with a good turn. How many good turns can you think of to do?

## Brownie World Pin

This is the Brownie World pin of the World Association of Girl Guides and Girl Scouts, which Brownies all over the world may wear. The two finger salute shows that Brownies in every country make the same Brownie Promise.

## The Troop Numeral

If your troop has a troop numeral, which gives the number of your troop, you wear it on your left sleeve.

# You Help Run the Troop

THIS IS your troop. If there are only eight or nine of you, or a full troop of sixteen girls, it takes every one of you to make it a good troop. Your leaders help you all the time but each one of you does her part as a member so everybody will have a happy time together.

You tell what you think is fun to do but you listen to the other girls and are willing to do what they want to do, too. You help plan what the whole troop will like. All of you and the leaders plan together. You learn to vote for what you think is best for the troop. A little time is needed at each meeting to attend to the business of the troop.

Talk about things that need to be done at every meeting and choose someone to do it each week or for three or four meetings. These are some of the jobs:

You get the room ready for the meeting.

See that it is cleaned up before you leave.

Mark attendance in the troop record book.

Collect the troop dues and give the money to the leader to keep for the troop.

You may want to have a hostess or two for each meeting. Decide what they are to do. Your troop may think of other jobs to be done. Everybody takes turns doing the jobs. You do the ones that are not so much fun as well as the ones you like best. Brownies work and play fair.

The troop talks about what you may need money for beside your national membership dues. Your leader explains a budget to you and shows you how to make and use one. You decide together what your troop dues should be every week. They may be a penny or two or a nickel or a dime. You may save your national membership dues for next year in the troop treasury. You learn what the treasurer's job is and elect a treasurer for the troop.

You learn to work in committees. When you are getting ready for a party, you may have one committee to write the invitations, one to decorate the room, one to serve refreshments, one to plan the games. You decide on what committees you need. Your leader tells you how a committee works.

Each committee is responsible for its part of the work. You are responsible for your share in whatever your committee is doing. Do you know what being responsible means? It is a good word for Brownies to learn and a good thing for Brownies to be.

To be responsible means you can be depended on to do what you say you will do and that you do it as well as you can. It means that you try to do it yourself without asking someone else to do it for you.

As the troop gets older, you may want to elect officers and have regular business meetings to run the troop. You may elect a chairman, a secretary or scribe, and a treasurer for longer than one or two meetings. Your leader will tell you what each officer does. You may already know if you have been in a club at school.

When you are elected to be an officer, you do the best job you can. You do not have to be an officer to help run the troop. You help make the plans for the troop and do your part to carry them out. When you elect an officer, you vote for the girl you think will do the job best. Sometimes you will wish to vote for your best friend. Ask yourself who can do the best job and vote for the girl who can. Your friend will understand that you are being fair if you have to vote for another girl.

# Out-of-Doors

You KNOW what fun it is to play outdoors and go on walks and picnics. There are so many things to do and to find out that Brownies stay out-of-doors as much as they can. You and the other girls and your leader will think of many things you want to do. Here are a few you will enjoy doing with your troop and with your family.

## Things To Do

**1.** Talk about the kind of clothes you should wear out-of-doors and in the woods.

**2.** Learn how to walk in the woods.

Watch small animals move. See how they "freeze." Can you be this still? Walk softly so you can get close to little animals, birds, and insects.

**3.** Learn what a compass is and how to use one.

*Be sure N for North is under the point of the needle.*

**4.** Learn four woodcraft trail signs that the Indians and early woodsmen made with stones. Follow a trail. Lay a trail for others to follow. These trail signs mean:

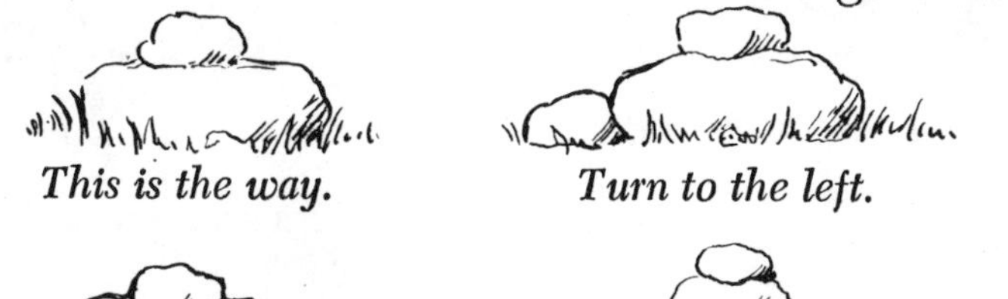

*This is the way.* *Turn to the left.*

*Turn to the right.* *Warning: Look for a message.*

## 5. Learn how to use a pocket knife.

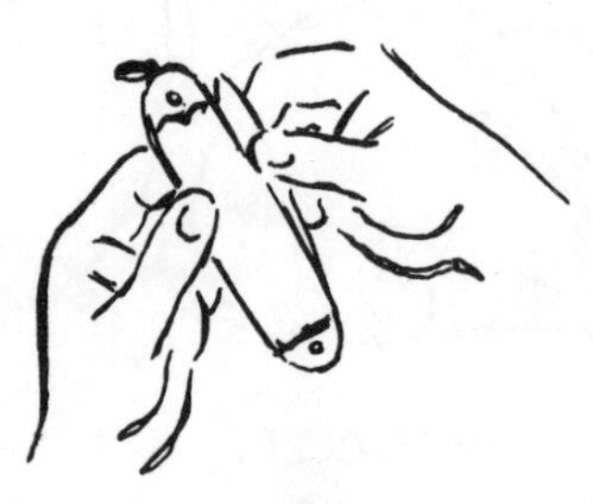

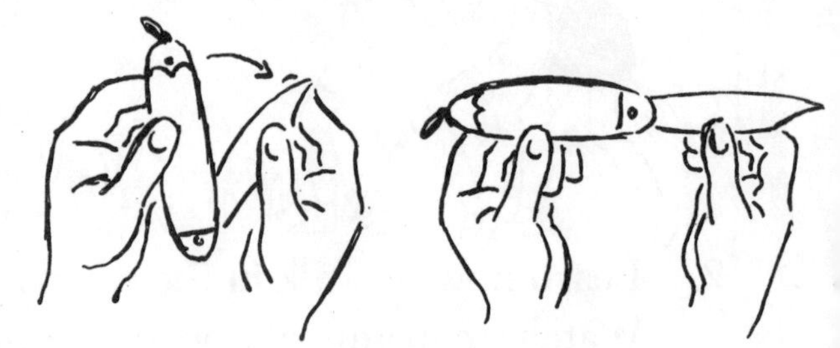

*Keep the fingers behind the blade.*

*Close the knife or hold it carefully by the blade to pass it to someone else.*

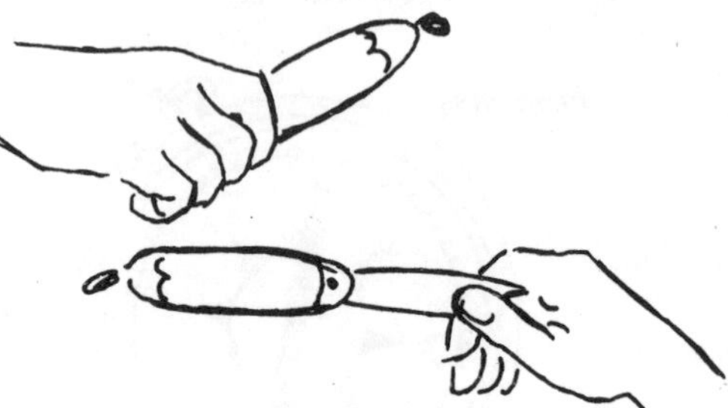

*Hold the knife like this.*

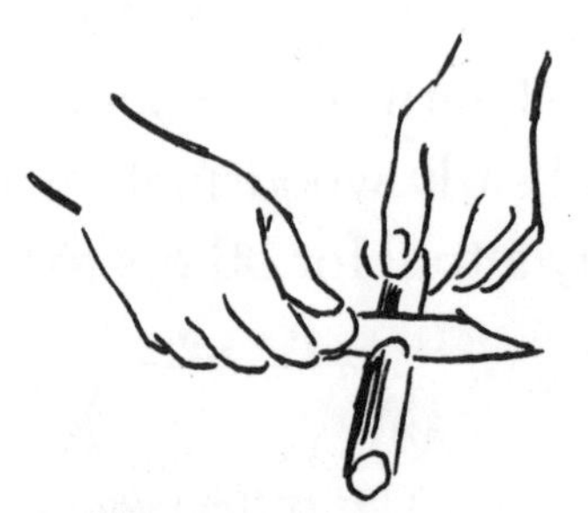

*Always cut away from your body.*

Never walk with an open knife in your hand.

6. Leave your picnic or outdoor play place clean.

Be sure that you have all your things.
Leave no scraps anywhere.
See that the gate is closed.

### More Things To Do

Play games out-of-doors. Help make an outdoor playhouse or a meeting place out-of-doors for the troop.

Go exploring around the block, in the park, and in the woods with your troop.

Help the troop plan a picnic and help carry out the plans.

Build a dam in a creek if you have permission.

Learn how to "stalk" and play stalking games.

After the troop has done many things together out-of-doors, your leaders will teach you how to build and take care of a fire, and how to put one out. You may learn to cook out-of-doors, too.

# Homemaking

Brownie Scouts have a good time keeping house at troop meetings. You learn how to do things to help other people, especially those at home. Make a list of the things you do to help at home. Here are some ways you can add to that list.

### Things To Do

**1.** Practice good housekeeping in the Brownie troop room. How many of the jobs in the picture can you do at home?

**2.** Play with your little brother or sister. They will enjoy the games and rhymes and songs you liked when you were that age. It is fun to make shadow pictures

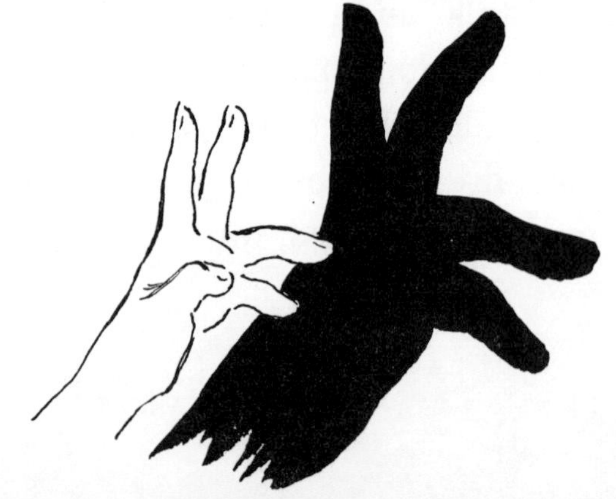

with your hands and handkerchief dolls for younger children.

*Use a large handkerchief.*

*Tie knots in corners 1 and 2 like this.*

*Pull the handkerchief between the knots together to make the head. Put a rubber band around it.*

*Put another rubber band on and pull the handkerchief up to make the body. Pull the handkerchief together in the back for the dress.*

**3.** Help take care of your clothes.

**4.** Learn to use kitchen utensils.

Peel an apple so you won't cut yourself or waste the apple.

Cut vegetables or bread on a board.

Learn to stir without spattering.

Be sure the handles of pots and pans on the stove are turned so they will not be over the edge of the stove.

When you are cooking, put the spoon you use in a saucer so you won't get the stove messy.

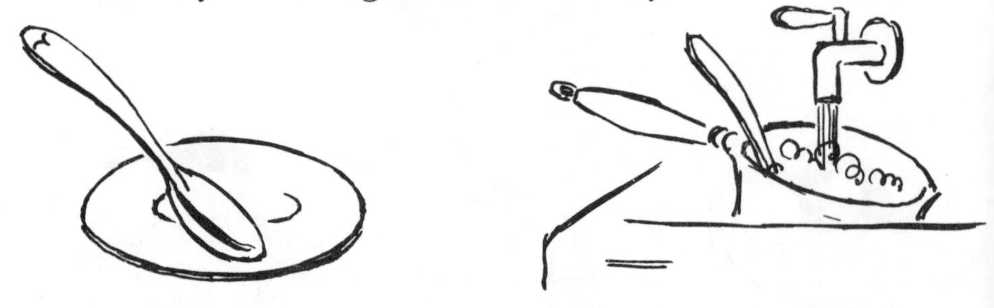

Put the saucepan or kettle you have used to soak.

**More Things To Do**

Learn how to introduce people, how to receive guests, how to serve refreshments.

Learn how to set the table correctly, how to wash dishes, how to make a bed.

Plan a party with the troop and help carry out the plans.

Learn how to press your hair ribbons and to iron an apron.

Learn how to make sandwiches, lemonade, cocoa, gingerbread, a good stew.

Prepare and pack your lunch for school, a hike, or a picnic.

Learn how to use a recipe in a cookbook.

Learn how to clean the stove and the refrigerator.

# *Music and Dancing*

Do you remember the rhyme you knew when you were small?

*Rings on her fingers, and bells on her toes,*
*She shall have music wherever she goes.*

Brownies have music at their troop meetings. And you have such a good time dancing, you feel as if you have bells on your toes too.

You learn songs and dances and play singing games. You enjoy listening to beautiful music, too, and learning something about great musicians. You may like to make up songs and dances yourself.

### Things To Do

**1.** Learn a song that has action to go with it. "Here We Go 'Round the Mountain" is a good one. You can find it in a book of singing games called *Skip to My Lou.*

**2.** Listen to five musical instruments and learn how they sound. Learn to tell what they are when you hear them on the radio.

**3.** Make a musical instrument and learn to play on it. You can play a tune through paper on a comb.

You can make a drum out of a keg, a large can, or an oatmeal box with a piece of old inner tube and some heavy string.

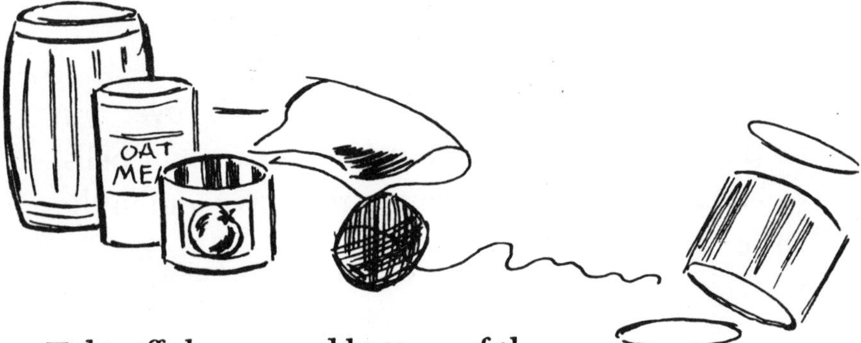


Take off the top and bottom of the can.

Paint the outside of the can to look like a drum. You might copy an Indian drum, or draw anything you like.

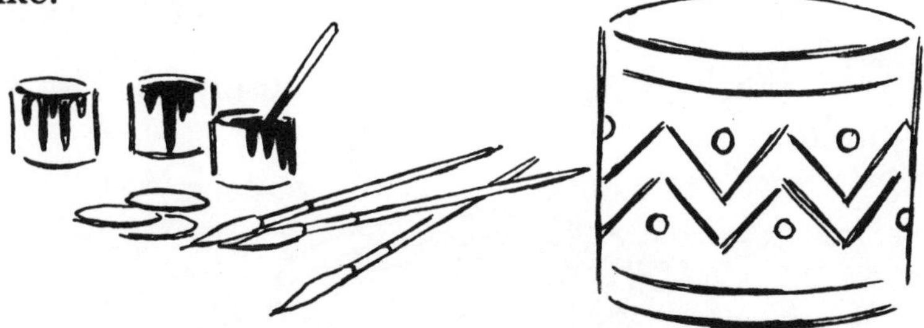

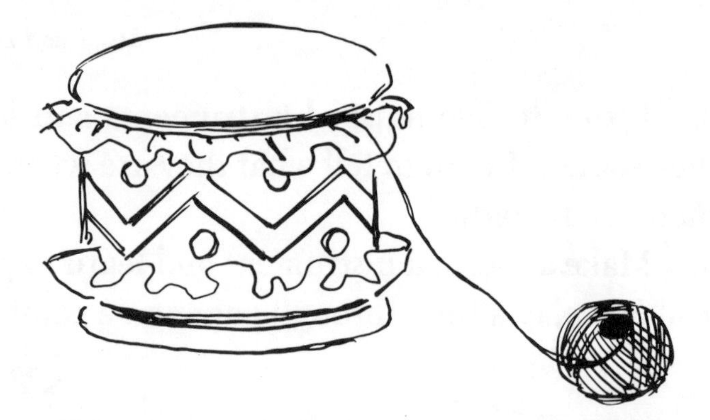

Stretch the rubber over the ends of the can and wind the string around and around.
Two smooth sticks will do for drumsticks.

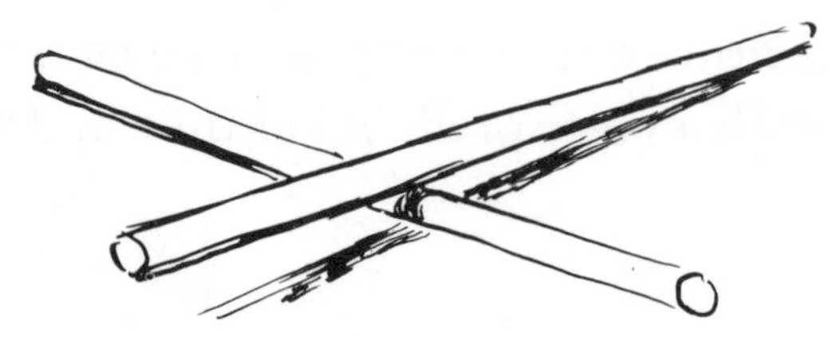

You can make a tambourine out of a tin-can cover or a pie pan, string, and soda-bottle tops or small bells.
Have holes punched in the rim of the cover and in the bottle tops.

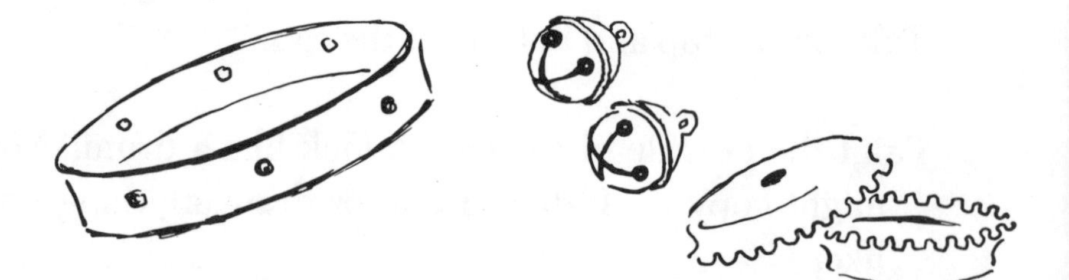

Tie the bottle tops or bells to it loosely so they will jingle.

**4. Listen to the musical sounds in nature.**

**5. Learn a simple folk dance.**

*Little Red Handkerchief — a Czechoslovakian folk dance*

6. Learn to lead a song.

**More Things To Do**

Act a song that has a story in it.

Play singing games at troop meetings.

Learn folk songs and folk dances that come from different parts of the United States.

Learn folk songs and folk dances from other countries.

Learn something about these musicians and listen to some of the music they wrote: Humperdinck, Prokofiev, Mozart, Grieg, MacDowell.

# Our Community

YOUR COMMUNITY is the neighborhood of homes, school, and stores that you live in. Often the whole town or city is spoken of as the community. Sometimes several farms that are near each other are called a community.

The people who live in a community are responsible for the kind of place it is. They are citizens of the community. What can you do to be a good citizen in your home, at school, in your Brownie troop, and in your community?

## Things To Do

**1.** See how many things you can find that your community provides to make you safe and happy. Here are a few.

**2.** Draw a map of your own neighborhood.

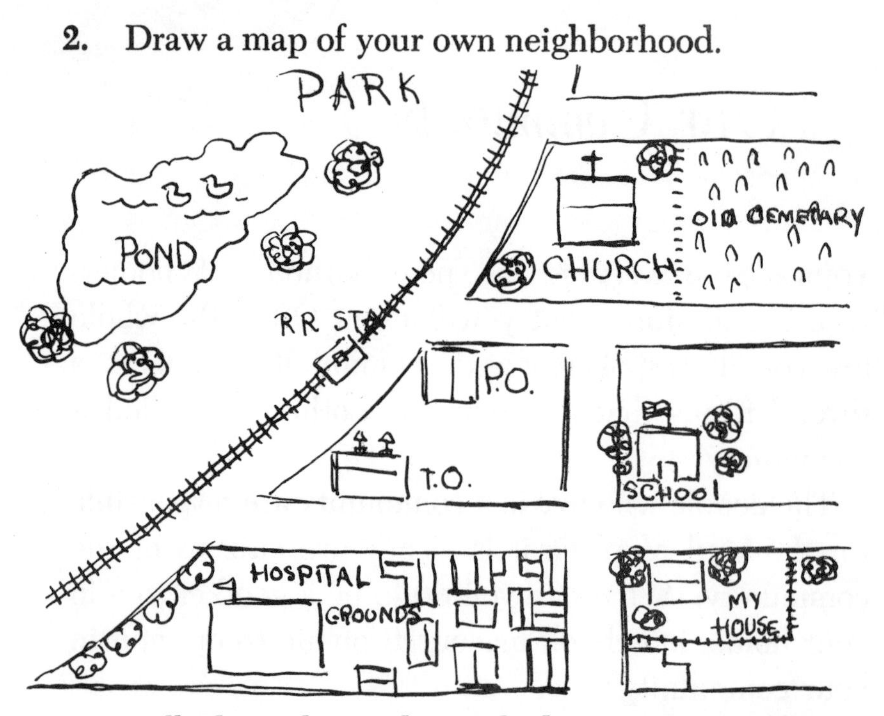


**3.** Talk about the work people do in your community. Where do they work? Your troop may visit some of these places. What are some of the jobs women do?

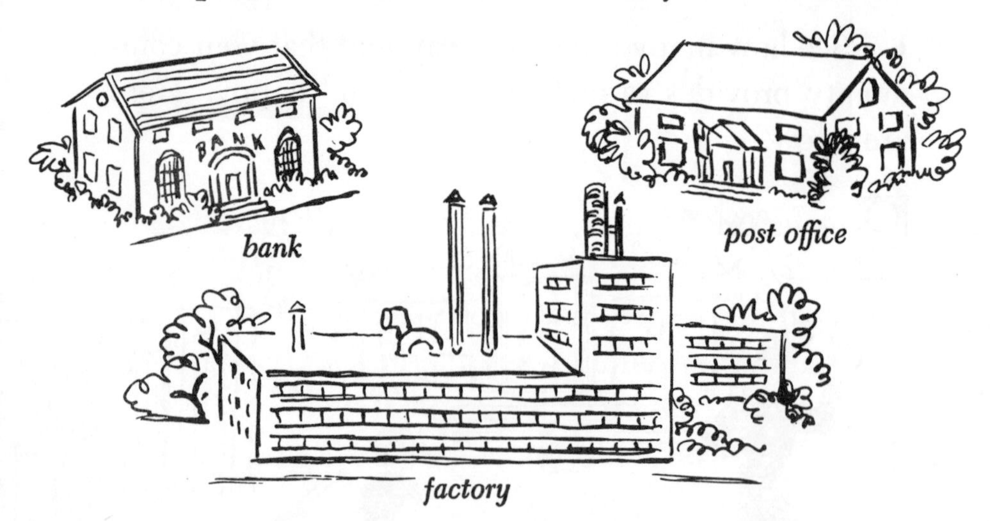


*bank*

*post office*

*factory*

4. Learn the history of the flag of the United States of America. Talk about what it stands for and find out which star stands for your state. Perhaps your troop can have a flag of your own.

5. Learn what is meant by respect to the flag and how to use it.

The flag should never touch the ground.

The flag of the nation always flies above any other flag used with it.

When the flag is used for decoration it is always hung with the stars in the upper left-hand corner like this:

It is never draped and never has anything placed on it.

When the flag gets too old and worn out to use, it should be burned, not thrown away.

You stand at attention when the flag is passing by or when it is raised or lowered. If you are in your Brownie Scout uniform, you salute.

**6.** Learn to take part in a flag ceremony. You show your respect to the flag by standing straight and quiet and still.

First, choose a color guard. This means one girl, called the color bearer, to carry the flag, and two guards to walk on each side of the bearer. If you have a troop flag, you need another bearer.

Everybody taking part in the ceremony stands at attention. The troop may be in a half circle, a horseshoe, or a square. The leader says, "Color guard, forward" and the three or four girls in the guard go to the flag and salute it. The troop flag is at the left of the United States flag.

The color bearers bring the flag and the troop flag on its left to the front of the troop. One guard is on each side of the color bearers.

The color guard stands still all through the ceremony. The rest of the troop salute the flag, give the Pledge of Allegiance, repeat the Brownie Scout Promise, sing or do whatever is planned for the ceremony.

When it is over, the leader says, "Color guard, dismissed." They turn and walk back together. After the bearer puts the flag back, they salute again and the ceremony is over.

## More Things To Do

Learn something about the history of your community. What Indians lived here and how did they live? Where did the early settlers come from? Visit interesting places with your troop.

Find interesting stories about the part of the country you live in. Bring them to the troop meeting. Talk about other parts of the country. There are many books about our country and about the people who make America a good nation to live in. Your librarian will help you find them.

Talk about how different everybody is in the troop, at school, in your own family. Some have blue eyes, some brown, some have curly hair, some straight. Some like peanut butter and others don't. Some like to sew and others would rather cook.

Find out how interesting people are because they are different. Make friends with somebody at school or in your neighborhood who came from a different country, or worships God in a different way, or who belongs to a different race. You will find out how much you feel and think alike.

Talk about how Brownies can help other people. Find out with your leaders and the other girls about some service that is needed outside your own home that you might do at troop meetings.

# Games

AT BROWNIE MEETINGS you have a chance to play the games you like best. You learn new ones, too, and learn to be a better player. Sometimes you and the other girls make up your own games.

You take turns and play fair and enjoy the game whether your side wins or loses. You choose different partners and play on different sides and are friends with *all* the girls, not just the ones you know best.

You will think of many games to play.

### Things To Do

**1.** Tell the troop about games you like to play indoors and out and see if they like them. Play the ones they want to play too.

**2.** Here is an old game everybody used to play. Ask your grandmother if she played it.

***Run, Sheep, Run***

Divide the troop in two sides. Each side chooses a captain. The girls on one side are Sheep, and the others are the Hunters. You choose a place for the home base.

All the Hunters stand at the base and close their eyes until the Sheep hide. The captain of the Sheep does not hide. When all the Sheep are hidden, their captain says, "Ready."

The Hunters start to look for the Sheep. When they are away from the base and the captain thinks the Sheep can get home safely, she calls, "Run, Sheep, Run."

The Sheep run home and the Hunters try to catch them. Count the ones who get home. Then you change sides and the Hunters are the Sheep and take their turn to hide. The first Sheep are the Hunters this time and try to catch the Sheep. You count the ones who get home again. The side with the most Sheep home without being caught wins the game.

**3.** Learn how to make some of the things you need for games, such as beanbags, jigsaw puzzles, and bird or flower pictures pasted on cardboard for nature games. It is easy to make rings to play Ring Toss or Quoits.

Cut a piece of stiff, heavy rope about 12 inches long.

Put the two ends together evenly like this.

Wrap adhesive tape around the ends tightly to join them together.

Now you have a ring.

There are many games you can play with rings like this. In some you try to throw the ring over a peg. In

some you throw it over the hand of another player. She holds her arm straight and does not catch it in her hand. Like this:

### *Ring Toss Relay or Quoits*

This is a hard game and takes practice but it is fun when you learn to play it well.

Divide the troop in two sides. Each side lines up and each girl takes a number, 1, 2, 3, and so on. No. 1 in each line stands about six or eight feet in front of her own side and faces the line.

She throws the ring to No. 2. If No. 2 catches it on her arm, she runs to the thrower's place and No. 1 goes to the back of the line. No. 2 then throws it to No. 3 and so on, until everyone has had her turn and No. 1 is back at the head of the line. The side whose No. 1 girl is back in place first wins the game.

If the ring is dropped, the girl who does not catch it must pick it up and throw it back. The thrower must catch it and toss it to her again.

**4.** Learn quiet games such as Anagrams, guessing games, and Charades. This one is fun.

### *Gossip, or Telephone, or Message*

You sit in a circle and choose the person to start the message. She thinks of something interesting to say and whispers it to the girl on her right. The second girl whispers it to the one on her right and so on around the circle. The last girl tells what the message sounded like when it got to her.

**5.** Teach a game that you know to the other girls. Talk with your leader about how to play the game and how to teach it so you can explain it clearly. This is a good way to teach a game. Suppose you are teaching Fruit Basket Upset.

First, get the girls in a circle and explain the game. Tell them how to play:

Each girl chooses a fruit for her name.

One girl, who is It, stands in the center.

She has a fruit name but does not have a seat.

She makes two or three girls get up by calling out "Apple, Peach, Banana (or any that she wishes), exchange!" The girls with those names must change places and the girl who is It tries to get a seat when they move. If she says "Fruit Basket Upset," everybody has to take another seat. The one who is left out is It.

Be sure everybody understands what to do. Try it once before you start playing. Agree on the rules. Have them choose the one to be It, and then play the game.

## More Things To Do

Ask the librarian to help you find good game books in the library. You can find singing games, running games, quiet games, ball and beanbag games, games with partners or sides or teams, games from other countries.

Plan and help make your own troop book of the games you and the other girls like best.

Learn how to make and fly a kite. Perhaps your father or brother will help you. The troop might have a kite-flying party for your fathers.

Teach some of the games you learn at troop meetings to your sisters and brothers or the other children in your neighborhood.

# *Farm and Garden*

It is fun to pet a baby calf, feed the chickens, gather eggs, and help in the garden. Perhaps you live in a large city and do not have a chance to do these things. But there are many ways for a Brownie troop to find out how food grows in fields and gardens and to get acquainted with farm animals.

## Things To Do

**1.** Learn all you can about these five garden vegetables and how we use them.

2. Learn all you can about a cow. Why is she such a useful animal?

What kind of teeth does a cow have? How does she eat?

Why does she have horns? Where do they grow?

3. Plant flower or vegetable seeds in a pot, a window box, or in a row in the garden. Get the soil ready for

the seed, take care of the plants, and watch them grow. They need water, sunshine, and air.

*Put one or two small stones or bit of broken jar in bottom for drainage.*

*Fill pot nearly to top with garden soil.*

*Plant your seed.*

*Keep the plant in the sunshine and give it plenty of water.*

**4.** Farmers and gardeners have to watch the weather so they will know when to plant and gather vegetables, grain, fruit, and hay. Learn about these clouds and what they mean. Watch for them in the sky.

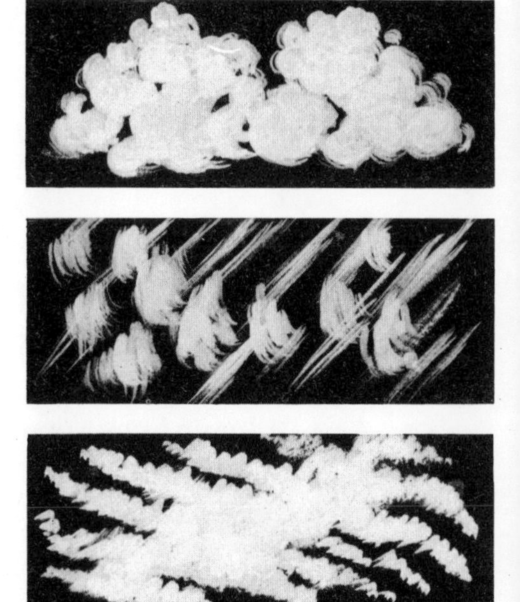

*cumulus or lamb's wool*

*mare's tails*

*mackerel sky*

## More Things To Do

Go with your troop or your family to visit a grain field, an orchard, a truck garden, a dairy farm. Find out all you can about what goes on there and who does the work.

Visit a nursery and see how plants that are to be put in a garden are started.

Learn how butter is made.

Find out what food products are raised and shipped from your part of the country.

# International Friendship

As a Brownie Scout you have friends all over the world who are Brownies too. You can learn about them at troop meetings. The best way for you and other Brownies to help bring about world friendship is to get along well with everybody you know in your neighborhood and at school, and to make new friends. Do you know someone in your community who came from another country?

**Things To Do**

**1.** Find out in what other countries there are Brownies. Learn to say the name they are called in their own country. Here are four and your leader knows many others.

Brownies are called *Poulakia* (Poo·laa′kia) in Greece.
It means Little Birds.

They are *Meiser* (May′ser) in Norway. That means Titmice.

They are *Kabouters* (Kah·baow′ters) in The Netherlands. That means Little Elves.

The native Brownies in South Africa are Sunbeams.

Read in your Brownie Equipment Catalog about the Brownie Doll set. It is a cut-out paper doll with Brownie uniforms from many countries in the World Association of Girl Guides and Girl Scouts.

**2.** Find out what countries your family and the families of other girls in the troop came from when they first came to America and learn all you can about them.

Have a treasure hunt in your own home and see how many things you can find that came from another country.

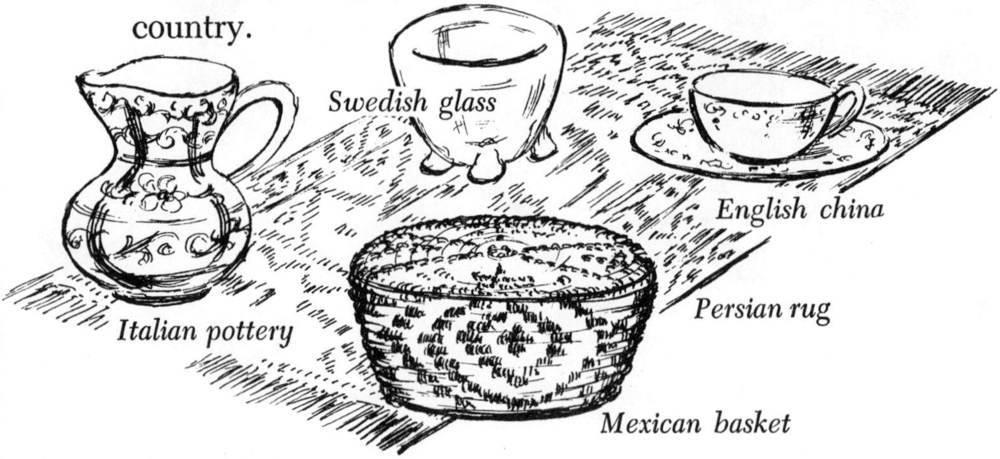

Swedish glass
English china
Persian rug
Italian pottery
Mexican basket

**3.** You have learned at school about how tulips grow in Holland and were brought to this country from there. Find out at school or in a book at the library what countries these flowers first came from.

Queen Anne's lace
hyacinth
chrysanthemum

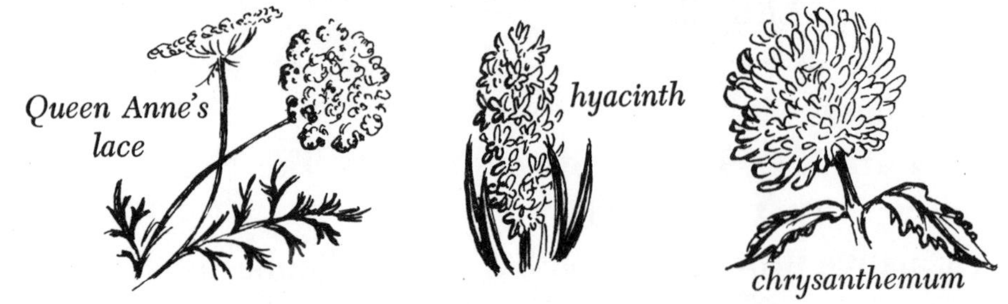

**4.** Talk about the United Nations at your troop meetings and all of you tell what you have learned about it. Do the countries you have studied at school belong to the United Nations? Are there Brownies in those countries? Try to find out some of the things the United Nations has done for children in the countries where they need help.

*This is the Girl Scout World Flag.*

Brownie Scouts are part of the world movement of Girl Guides and Girl Scouts and are friends all over the world. Our country belongs to the United Nations to help bring about world friendship.

Find out if there is a United Nations flag in your community. Who has it and when and where is it displayed? See it if you can.

*This is the United Nations flag.*

**More Things To Do**

Learn to say in another language such things as "How do you do," "Good night," "Please," "Thank you," "Merry Christmas," and other words.

Learn a rhyme or song in another language.

Learn folk songs, games, and folk dances of other countries and find out which country they came from.

Act a story from another country and make costumes to suit the story.

Find out about the food people eat in other countries. Talk about what you eat at home that comes from another country. Perhaps the troop can cook something that children in another country like.

Read about children who live in other lands. There are such good stories and pictures about them that you will feel you really know them and how they live in their own homes. You will find these books in the library.

# *Health and Safety*

YOU HAVE a better time and look prettier too when you know how to keep yourself well and strong. Brownies can be good citizens by practicing health and safety rules at troop meetings and all the time.

### Things To Do

1. Learn to read the weather thermometer.

At what temperature do you need a sweater? A coat and cap?

Why should you take off wraps in the house?
How does the weather tell you what to wear?

2. Learn why rest and sleep are important.
Watch a puppy rest.

How does a kitten rest?

Can you rest and sleep this well?

How and where do birds sleep?

What does "hibernate" mean? What animals hibernate and how do they get their food?

**3.** Plants, animals, and people must have food to live and grow. Learn why you need these seven kinds of food to grow up strong and healthy.

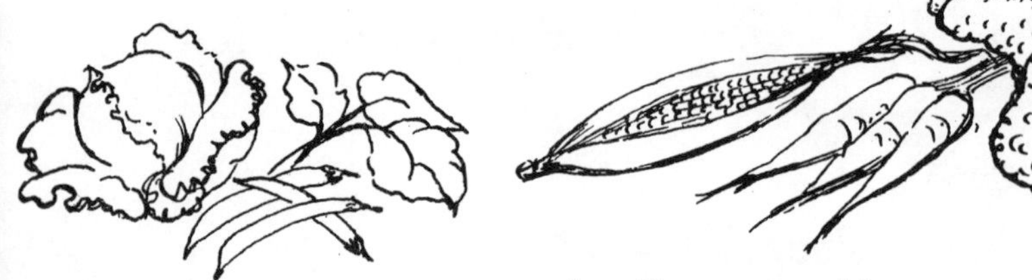

*green and yellow vegetables*

*oranges, grapefruit, and tomatoes*

*potatoes and other vegetables and fruit*

*milk and cheese*

*meat, eggs, poultry, and fish*

*bread and cereals*

*butter and margarine*

**4.** Plan a menu for a meal using these foods. Learn how to prepare and cook some of these foods at troop meetings. Help your mother cook some of them.

**5.** Talk at troop meetings about the ways you can practice safety at home, at school, on a hike, at play with small children, at the swimming pool, in winter, in summer.

## More Things To Do

Learn what a germ is. Talk at troop meetings about the harmful ones, such as a cold germ. What can you do to keep yourself and people around you from getting a cold?

Learn what to do if you or someone else gets hurt.

Help fill a first aid kit for the troop room. Decide with the other girls what should be in it. Learn what each thing is for and how to use it.

Prepare an attractive tray to serve a meal to a sick person.

Write a poem or story or song about keeping healthy or playing safely. Or make up a play about health or safety and act it at a troop meeting.

Look for books in the library about growing strong and healthy. You will find interesting stories about safety too.

Make a list of important telephone numbers, such as the fire department, the doctor, the gas company, and others.

# Nature

*The world is so full of a number of things,*
*I'm sure we should all be as happy as kings.*

When Robert Louis Stevenson wrote this in *A Child's Garden of Verses,* he must have been talking about the world out-of-doors.

Brownies find many things to make them happy and thankful. So much is going on in the world all about you that you can have an adventure at troop meetings and every day of your life.

It is exciting to learn about animals, birds and insects, flowers and trees, rocks, soil, weather, water, and stars out-of-doors. You can learn about them in the house, too. Nature is everywhere all the time—in cities, in the woods and fields, in the winter, spring, summer, and fall.

## Things To Do

**1.** In the spring, place twigs from trees or bushes in water in a sunny window and watch the buds unfold.

Be careful not to harm the plant when you snip the twigs.

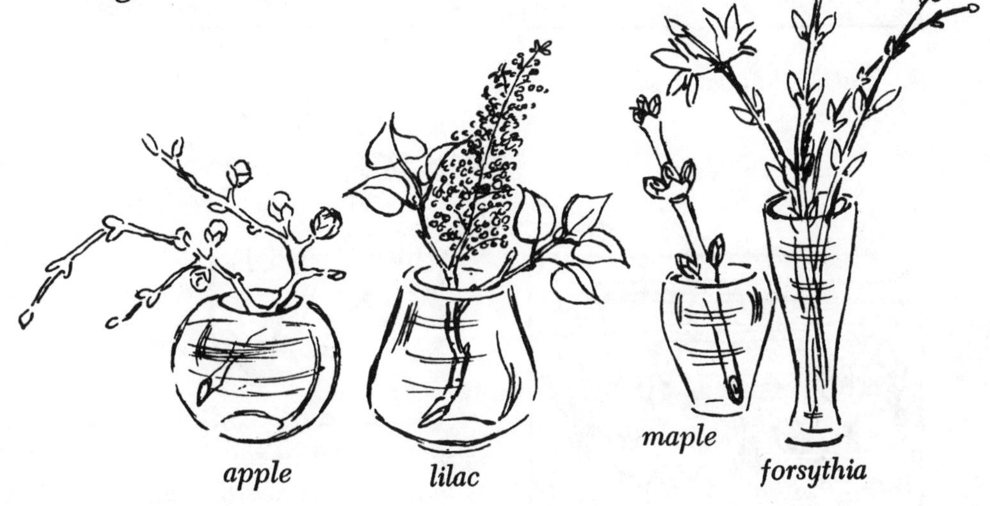


**2.** Plant an aquarium for goldfish or small tropical fish.

*Put sand and a few small stones in the bottom of the aquarium.*

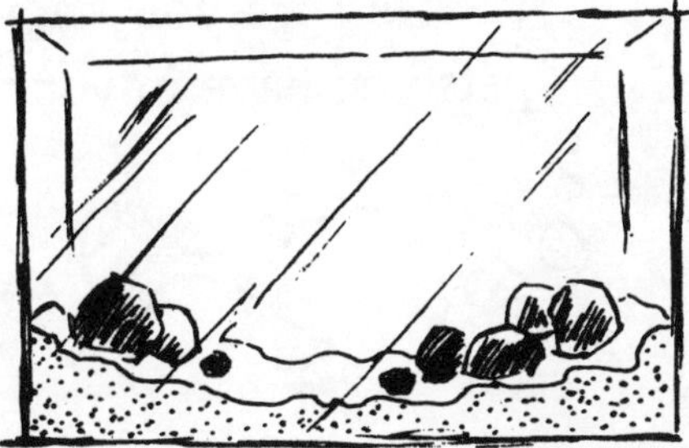

*Put a piece of cardboard in the bottom and pour water on it slowly so sand will not wash. Fill the aquarium about half full. The cardboard will rise to the top.*

*Put in the water plants.*

*Use the cardboard again and pour water in slowly until the aquarium is nearly full.*

Be sure you know how to feed and care for the pets you have in your aquarium.

3. Learn how animals, birds, and insects protect themselves.

*stinger*

4. Make a bird-feeding tray.

Get a flat board that can be fastened on the window sill. Nail strips of wood or molding around the edges so the seed won't blow off.

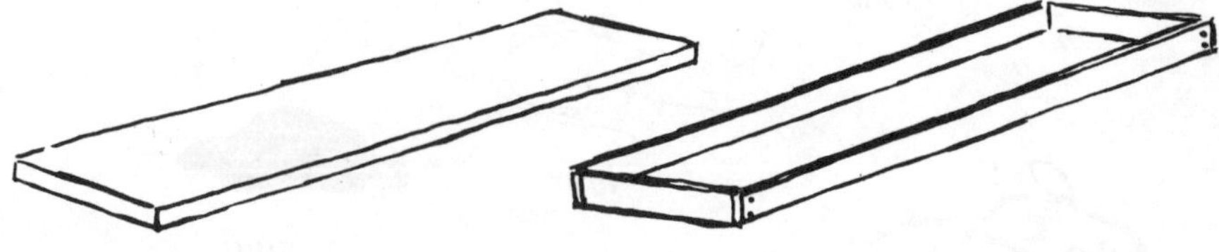

Put a nail at one or both ends to tie on a suet bag.

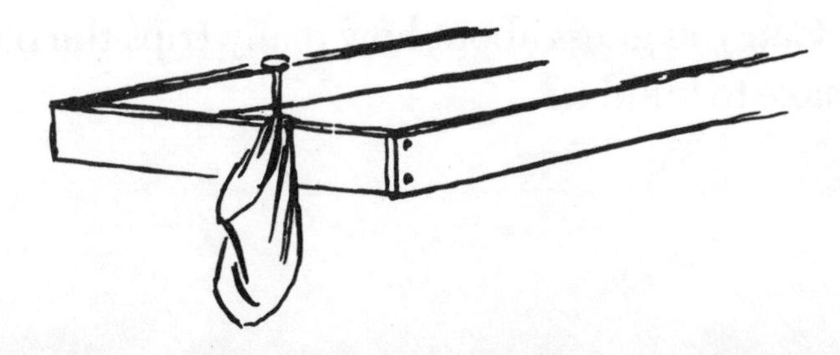

Fasten the board to the window sill.

**5.** Take a last year's bird's nest apart to see what the birds used to make it.

Can you guess about how many trips the birds had to make to build it?

**6.** Learn what poison ivy, poison oak, and poison sumac are. Why should you never touch them?

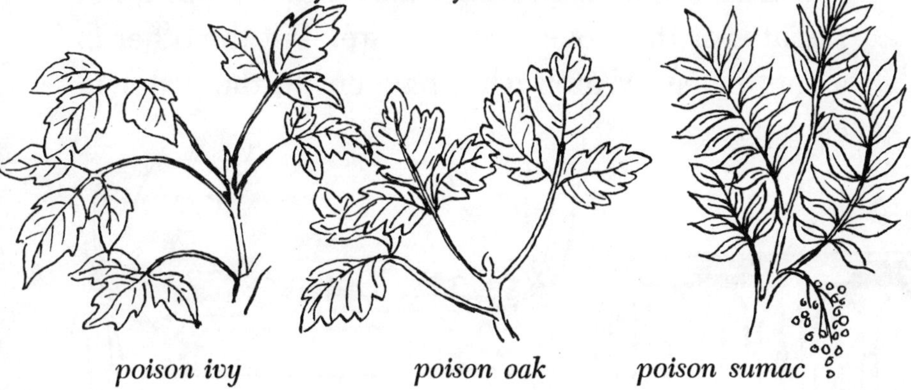


**7.** Look for animal tracks in the snow or damp earth.

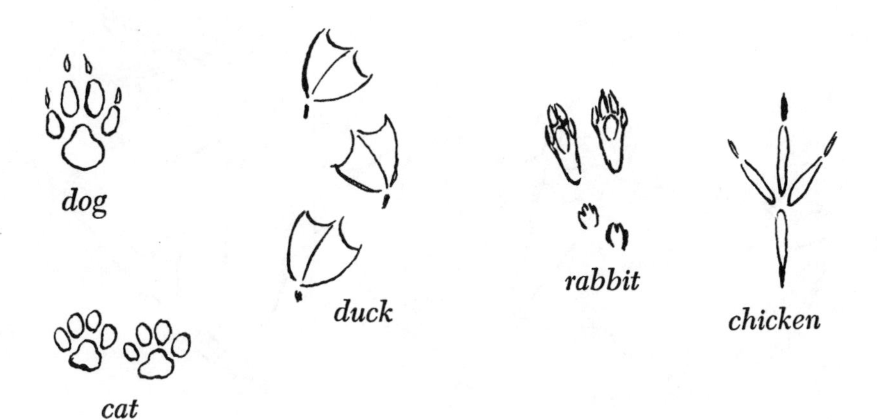


**8.** Do you know what makes it rain? Find out in books at the library and by asking questions at home and at school. Talk about it at troop meetings. Look at clouds and learn which ones mean rain.

Find out what heat does to water by doing this: Put a little water in two flat pans. Put one on a hot radiator or the stove or near a fire. Put the other in a cold place. Watch what happens to the water in each pan.

Notice how much faster wet clothes dry in the sun than in the shade.

## More Things To Do

Try to watch the same animals, birds, or insects long enough to learn something about them. Find an ant-hill and watch the ants at work. See how squirrels play, how they eat, and how they put away food for the winter. Watch birds build a nest and feed their babies. Watch a spider spin a web.

Learn all you can about your own pet. Take care of your pet.

Make a nature scrapbook or diary. Keep a record of what you see on nature walks. Write about it or sketch something you like or make a spatter print. You may write a nature story or poem.

Look for patterns in leaves, ferns, flowers, and snowflakes.

Learn five constellations. A constellation is a group of stars that make a picture in the sky.

Play nature games.

Find out what wild flowers in your part of the country should never be picked.

Look for the things you see in nature in nature books. Find the picture and learn the name of what you have seen. There are books about animals, trees, birds, turtles, flowers, weather—all the things you want to know. You can get them at the public library. Perhaps your troop can buy a few, too. Two special ones you will like are *In Woods and Fields*, by Margaret Waring Buck, and *Let's Find Out*, by Herman and Nina Schneider.

# *Arts and Crafts*

Do YOU like to draw and color and look at pictures? Most Brownie troops have pencils, crayons, paints, and drawing paper to use at troop meetings. You may want to draw something in the troop room or go outside to sketch what you see.

Brownies like to make things, too. You may make something you need to use in troop meetings and to help furnish the troop room. You make gifts for other people.

You learn about real crafts. You learn about the great artists and craftsmen who have made pictures and statues and pottery and lace and other beautiful things for people to use and enjoy. You can find many of these things in your own community.

## Things To Do

**1.** Make something out of clay. You need:

A piece of clay the size of your two fists.

A piece of linoleum or board to work on.

A small pan of water.

A small pan of "slip." Slip is clay mixed with water to the thickness of cream.

A rag.

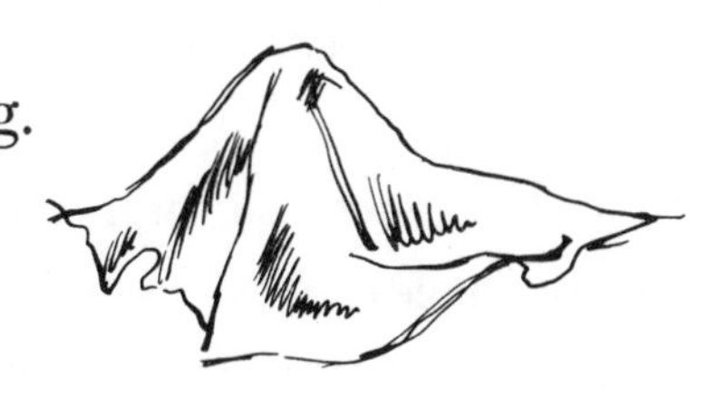

You can press and shape and twist your clay into anything you like. The body of many animals and birds is shaped like an egg. If you want to make an animal, you can divide your clay into pieces—the largest for the body and smaller ones for the head and tail and legs if you make them. Before you stick two pieces together, dip the two spots to be joined in the pan of slip. Then the leg or head won't fall off when it gets dry. When your clay gets dry or scratchy, dip your fingers in the pan of water and pinch it smooth again.

After you have made things out of clay, you may have a piece you like so well you want to keep it or give it to someone as a present. The troop may go with your leader, or your father may take you to a kiln to learn about pottery and to get your piece fired.

**2.** Make a notebook for yourself. You may use it for a nature notebook, for your sketches, poems, and stories, or anything you like.

You will need cardboard. It may be heavy or you may use the back of a school tablet. You need a ruler, scissors, pencil, paste, drawing paper—any color you choose—a pretty piece of cloth for the cover, blank paper for the pages and something to fasten the book together.

If you use a tablet back, you can staple the book together. If your cardboard is heavy, you will have to get holes punched in it. You can put it together with chicken rings. They are easy to find and do not cost much.

This is how you make the book.

Cut the cardboard to the size you want.

Cut the cloth for the cover two inches longer and two inches wider than the cardboard so you can turn it down all around the edges.

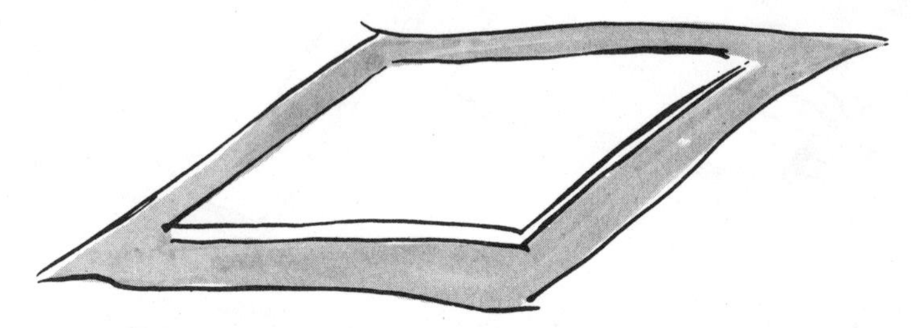

Paste the cloth on one side of the cardboard smoothly, turning the corners neatly and pasting the edges of the cloth on the other side.

Cut your drawing paper large enough to cover the cloth edge about half an inch. Paste it on carefully.

When you have made both covers and cut your pages to go in the book, put them together. If the cardboard is light, staple the book together in three places about half an inch from the edge like this:

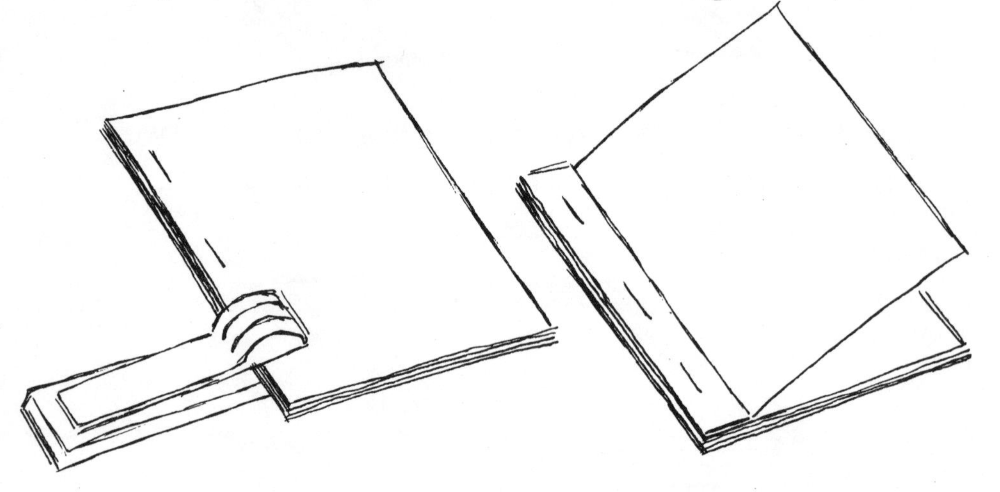

Bend the covers carefully about an inch from the edge. If you use heavy cardboard, get three holes punched in the cover and all the pages about half an inch from the edge. Fasten the book together with chicken rings.

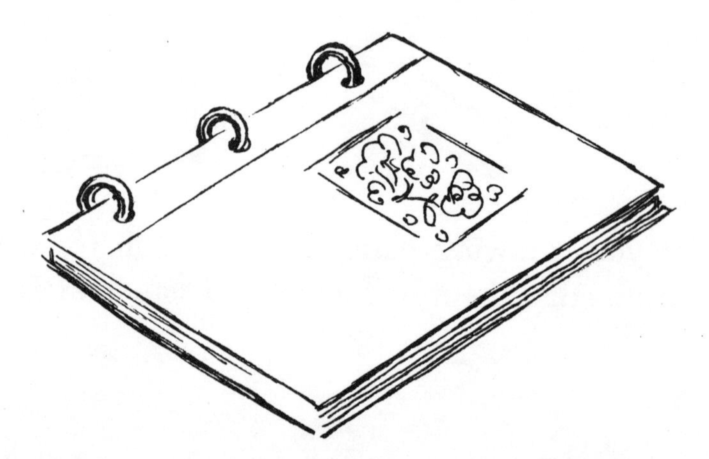

**3.** Make a reed and raffia mat. You need:

*a raffia needle* *raffia* *reed*

Soak the reed in warm water for five or ten minutes. Cut one end of the reed on a long slant.

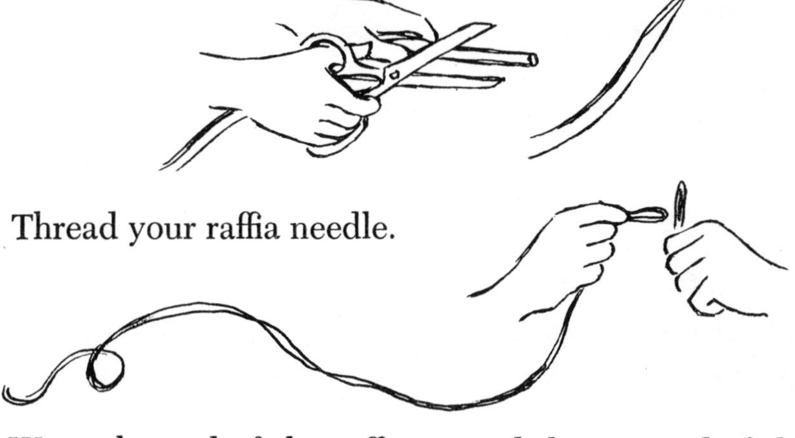

Thread your raffia needle.

Wrap the end of the raffia around the cut end of the reed for about an inch.

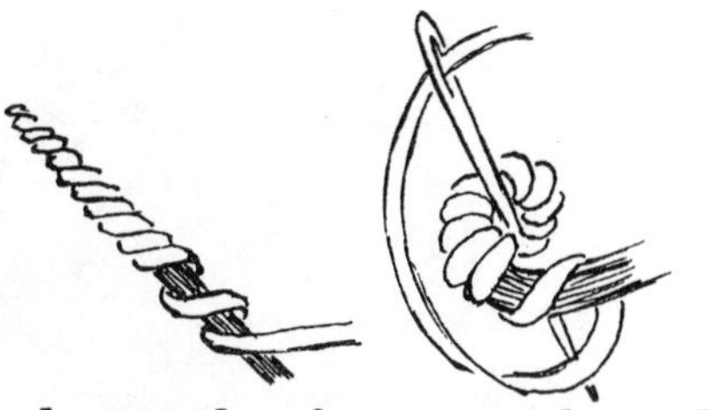

Coil this inch of wrapped reed and take one or two stitches in last coil to keep it in place.

Keep on wrapping and coiling and stitching until the mat is the size you want.

To finish, cut the end of the reed on long slant and wrap and stitch it tightly into the mat with raffia.

If you like this, you can learn to make baskets.

**4. Make a Christmas tree.**

**Here is a pattern copied from a wooden Christmas tree made in Vienna. You need heavy cardboard, scissors or knife, pencil, paper, and poster paint.**

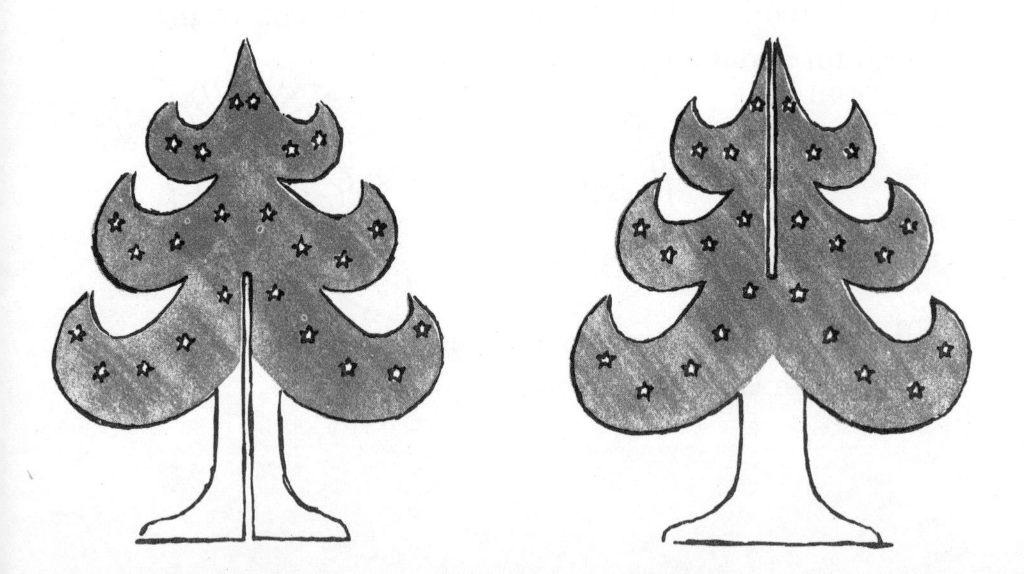

Copy the pattern on your paper.
Make your pattern five or six inches high.
Trace the pattern on the heavy cardboard.
Cut the pieces carefully so the tree will stand when put together.
Paint and decorate the tree with poster paint.

The tree can be made of wood if you can use a jigsaw. Softwood such as balsa, white pine, or poplar is best.

**5.** Make a spatter print for your nature notebook. You need:

Paper thick enough to absorb ink or poster paint; a toothbrush; a nail file, tongue depressor, or wooden picnic spoon; straight pins. You may need an apron. Select a leaf you like. This is a sycamore leaf.

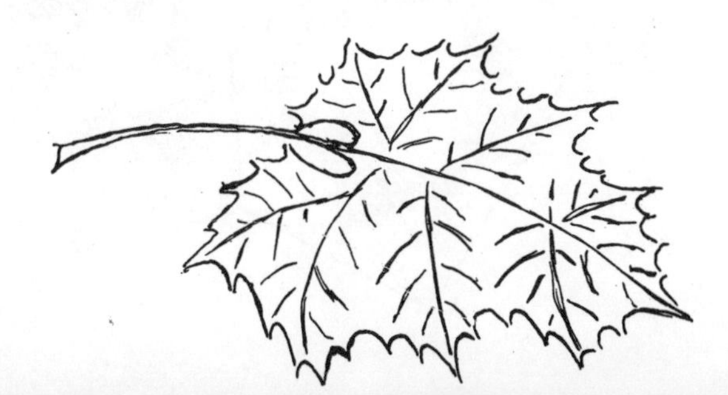

Fasten the leaf to the paper carefully with pins to show the outline of the leaf.

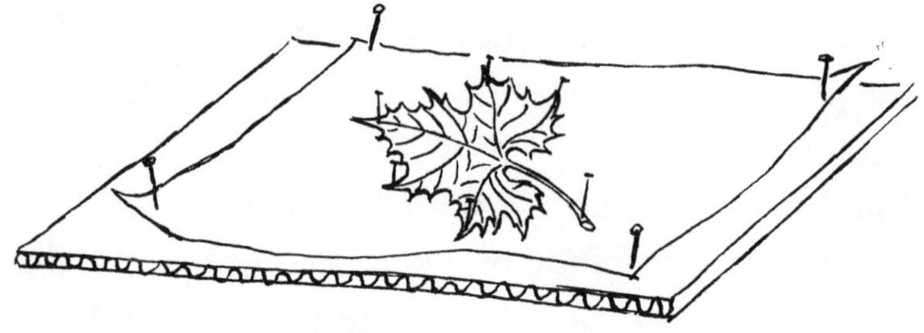

Put the ink or paint on your brush with the tongue depressor so you won't get too much.

Scrape the tongue depressor lengthwise over the brush *toward you* so the bristles will spatter the ink *back down* on the paper and not on your clothes.

Let it dry a little and take out the pins. Wait a little longer and take off the leaf. Let it get really dry before you touch it.

It will look like this.

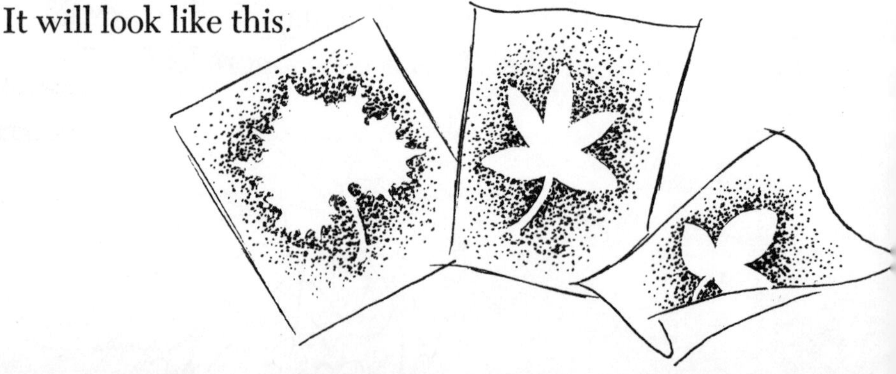

You can learn other ways to make spatter prints. You may brush the ink over a piece of wire screen, or you may use a spray gun instead of a toothbrush.

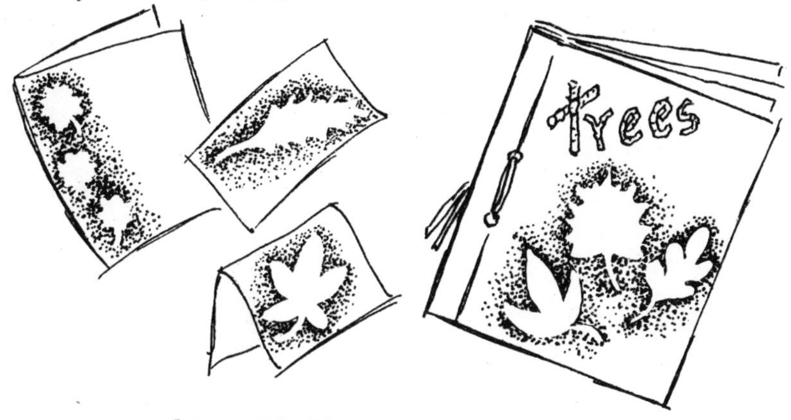


**More Things To Do**

With the other girls plan a mural or frieze for your troop room. You can fasten wide brown wrapping paper to the walls with Scotch tape or thumbtacks. All of you can draw the pictures you plan. It may be easier to work on the floor and then put up the mural.

Draw pictures to go with a story you hear or read. Draw what you feel when you are listening to music.

Look for different colors, lines, and patterns in the woods. Draw some of the patterns you find. Learn what a design is and how to make one. Make a design for something you see or imagine.

Learn how to make a stencil and use your design.

Learn how to weave with yarn on a small cardboard or wooden frame. Make pot holders or dishcloths for gifts.

# Books and Plays

Heidi

*A book, I think, is very like*
*A little golden door*
*That takes me into places*
*Where I've never been before.*
*It leads me into fairyland*
*Or countries strange and far.*
*And best of all, the golden door*
*Always stands ajar.*

BY ADELAIDE LOVE

WHAT KINDS of stories do you like best? What is your favorite book? Do you like to write stories and poems yourself? At Brownie meetings you often hear and tell and act stories. Sometimes you may help write a play and give it for the troop. You use books to find out things you want to know.

### Things To Do

**1.** Plan and have a storybook party. Dress as your favorite book character.

2. Treat your books well and they will last a long time.
Open a book so it will not break or tear.

Use a bookmark instead of leaving a book open like this.

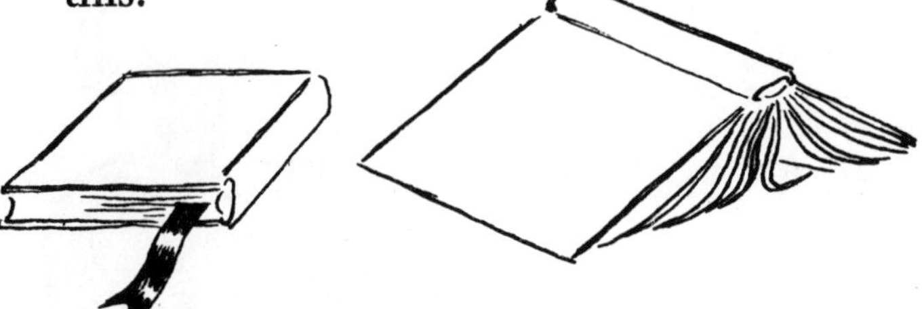

Put a book away when you are not reading it.
Keep books clean.

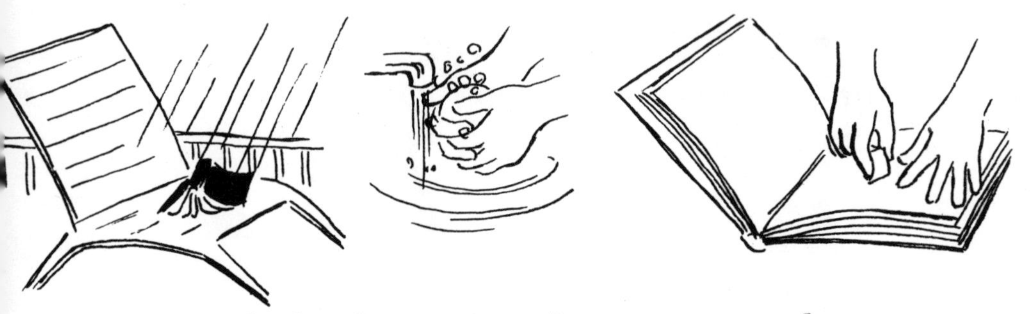

3. Make hand puppets and give a puppet show.

***Cardboard Puppets***

Decide on your story and cut out pictures or draw the characters you need. Use these for patterns and trace them on stiff cardboard. Cut the figures out. Cut strips of cardboard about three or four inches long and nearly an inch wide. Tack or glue one on to each figure to use as a holder.

***Finger Puppets***

It is easy to make finger puppets. You can use a doll's head or make a head. You use your hand for the body. Put your first finger in the neck and use your middle finger for one arm and your thumb for the other.

You can make a head out of a paper bag with a face drawn on it, out of a potato or an apple with a hole in it, and out of clay. Wool yarn makes good hair.

For clothes you can use a doll's dress or a piece of cloth with slits cut for armholes. Button or tie the dress around the neck or around your finger where it goes into the head. Pull the dress down around your hand.

*doll puppet*

*paper bag puppet*

*potato puppet*

Use a box or table for the stage. The girls moving the puppets get down behind the table and hold the puppets so their hands will not show. Move the puppets to act the story. You may talk for your own puppet, or someone else may tell the story as you move the puppets around.

## More Things To Do

Visit the public library and learn how to find the books you want.

Learn to look things up in the dictionary and the encyclopedia, and in books about nature and other subjects.

Plan with the other girls and the leader to start a library for your Brownie troop. You may lend each other your favorite books. You may decide to use part of the troop budget to buy some books you want.

Read and tell stories to your younger brothers and sisters.

Act stories you and the other girls like.

Write a play with some of the girls in the troop and give it for the rest of the troop.

# *Special Girl Scout Days*

EVERYBODY likes to celebrate special days—Christmas, Hanukkah, Valentine's Day, Easter, Halloween, Thanksgiving, your own birthday. Girl Scouts have some special days to celebrate. When your troop plans what you are going to do, mark these dates on your calendar.

**Founder's Day—October 31**

Mrs. Low was born on October 31 and Girl Scouts celebrate her birthday as Founder's Day. She said she was glad she was born on Halloween, when everybody has fun, because it gave her a good reason to play with girls all her life.

## Girl Scout Week

Girl Scout Week starts on the Sunday before the Girl Scout Birthday—March 12. The birthday of the first Girl Scout troop is so important that we celebrate the whole week the birthday comes in instead of just one day. Brownie Scouts go to church or synagogue in uniform with their families or with the troop on Girl Scout Sunday. You celebrate the Girl Scout Birthday at the troop meeting that week. You try especially hard every day that week to help your families at home.

## The Girl Scout Birthday—March 12

Mrs. Low started the first Girl Scout troop in Savannah, Georgia, on March 12, 1912. This day is called the Girl Scout Birthday and is celebrated by Brownie and Girl Scout troops all over the United States.

Many troops collect money for the Juliette Low World Friendship Fund on the Girl Scout birthday. Mrs. Low wanted Girl Scouts and Girl Guides—as they are called in some countries—to learn to know each other and to be friends. After she died, the Girl Scouts thought the best way to do something in her memory was to carry on this work she started. The Juliette Low World Friendship Fund is money given by every Brownie and Girl Scout, even if it is only a little, to do this. Your leader will tell you how the money is spent.

## Thinking Day—February 22

February 22 is the birthday of Lord Robert Baden-Powell, the Founder of Scouting for boys and girls all over the world. It is the birthday of his wife, Lady Baden-Powell, too. She is the Chief Guide in the World Association of Girl Guides and Girl Scouts. When you become a member of the Girl Scouts in your own country, you become a part of the world movement.

We celebrate the Baden-Powells' birthday by thinking about our sister Guides and Scouts all over the world, and about what it means to be friends with them. It is called Thinking Day.

## Your Troop Birthday

The troop birthday is a very special day for Brownie Scouts. This is the registration day for your troop at the National Headquarters of the Girl Scouts. Every year you and the other Brownies in the troop bring your national membership dues to your leader in time to be sent in before that day. Then you get your new membership cards.

It is fun to have a real birthday party in the month you re-register. You might have a cake and candles for the troop. Some troops have a special ceremony and have their new membership cards given to them. Or you might get your membership star, which means you have been a member for a year, and fasten it on your pocket that day.

# Getting Ready To Fly Up

WHEN YOU are nine years old or in the fourth grade, you are getting ready to take your next step in Girl Scouting—from being a Brownie Scout to going on as an Intermediate Girl Scout.

You will do many of the same things you enjoy as a Brownie, but you will do them differently as you grow older and will learn many new exciting ones. You will make the larger Girl Scout Promise and subscribe to the Girl Scout Laws. Your leader will tell you what "subscribe" means. You will have more responsibility for running the troop. You will have requirements to meet.

Because you are already a member of the Girl Scouts, you meet the Tenderfoot requirements for the Intermediate Girl Scout troop while you are still a Brownie. You and the other girls who are going on will probably spend most of the last three or four months in your Brownie troop meetings getting ready. Your leader will help you.

Now you want to get the *Girl Scout Handbook* to use instead of this one. It tells you how to meet the requirements. It is full of interesting things you will do as a Girl Scout for the next four years.

When you have met all the Tenderfoot requirements and are ready to make the Girl Scout Promise, you will have another ceremony like the Investiture when you became a Brownie Scout.

This is called the fly-up ceremony and you get a pair of wings embroidered in gold to sew on your new green uniform. Your wings show that you have been a Brownie Scout and have flown up instead of being a new member.

When you make the Girl Scout Promise, you are invested with the Girl Scout pin. You can look forward to continued good times in your troop and greater opportunities to "Be Prepared" as you go on in Girl Scouting.

PDD 12-51
6-59